DAY 1

About The Author

Paul Stamp is a former printer and website publisher, Paul has always had a knack for storytelling and communication. His journey into the world of addiction support began when he recognized his own struggles. This realization ignited a desire to make a difference, prompting him to delve into a personal Diary, that eventually turned into a book

Paul's writing is infused with empathy and understanding, as he draws from both personal experiences and the stories of those he has helped. He believes that everyone deserves a second chance and that recovery is possible with the right support and resources. His work aims to provide hope, encouragement, and practical advice for individuals and families navigating the challenging path of addiction.

In addition to his writing, Paul is actively involved in his local Brass band scene and has a strange passion for Flugelhorns.

When he's not writing or supporting others, Paul enjoys exploring the scenic beauty of Yorkshire, spending time with his family, and engaging in various outdoor activities. He believes that nature and exercise play a vital role in healing and often incorporates elements of the great outdoors into his recovery philosophy.

Connect with Paul

Paul invites readers to join him on this journey of healing and hope. Whether you are seeking support for yourself or a loved one, his work aims to inspire and empower. For more information and resources or to connect, please visit his website: **https://soberdayone.com/** or https://www.facebook.com/groups/soberdayone.

Table of Contents

About The Author 2

Preface 6

Day 1 9

    Alcohol Island 9

Day 2 17

    Full Swing 17

Day 3 21

    The Dream 21

Day 4 26

    Bullseye 26

Day 5 30

    Bert 30

Day 6 - 7 35

Peugeot 35

Day 8 40

    Bananaman 40

Day 9 44

    Aiwa 44

Day 10 49
  Wonka 49
Day 11 - 15 55
  Honeymoon 55
Day 16 61
  Jog on 61
Day 17 66
  Canal 67
Day 18 74
  Numb 75
Day 19 - 23 82
  The Clock 82
Day 24- 30 89
  Berts silence 89
Golden Rules 90
Conclusion 94

Preface

I never set out to write a book. Honestly, if you had told me months ago that I'd be sitting here, writing this, I would have laughed—probably with a pint in my hand.

I intended to write something just for myself—a personal log—a raw, unfiltered account of my journey, something I could look back on when I needed a reminder not to go back to drinking. It was meant to be a private commitment, a way to hold myself accountable.

But then a thought struck me—What if I document the entire process?

Not just the first step, not just the misery of Day One, but everything. The cravings, the withdrawal, the moments of doubt, the small victories, and—hopefully—the transformation. What if I could capture the highs and lows of breaking free from alcohol in a way that wasn't clinical or preachy but real?

And so, this book was born.

This is not a polished self-help manual. There are no "12 easy steps to sobriety" here. No lectures, no scientific jargon, no judgment. Just the honest, messy, and sometimes painfully humorous journey of one ordinary person—me—who decided to row away from Alcohol Island.

If this book helps just one person break free, if it gives hope to someone stuck in that never-ending cycle of "I'll quit tomorrow," then every word will have been worth it because I know how it feels to be trapped. To wake up exhausted, ashamed, and wondering how the hell you let it get this far. To promise yourself that tonight will be different—only to find yourself reaching for another drink. To look in the mirror and not recognize the person staring back at you.

But here's the truth: You are not trapped. The door has been open all along—you just have to take the first step through it.

And that's where Day One comes in.

Day One is the hardest. It's the wall that keeps so many people from ever starting. The moment when your mind tries to convince you that it's impossible. **It's not too bad since you can always quit later.**

But here's something I urge you to do on your Day One—something that will become your anchor when things get tough:

Take a photo of yourself. Not to shame yourself but to see yourself. One day, you'll look back at that picture and barely recognize the person in it.

Write down your reasons for quitting. Not a list of "why drinking is bad" vs. "why quitting is good." Your real reasons. The ones that hit deep. The ones you don't say out loud. Maybe it's your health. Maybe it's the look in your child's eyes. Maybe it's because you're just tired of feeling like this. Write it down. You're going to need it.

I invite you to read my Day One and then write or record your own. Do it now, before doubt creeps in.

Because here's what I've learned: Sobriety isn't about giving something up. It's about getting your life back. It won't be easy. But I promise you, the life waiting on the other side is worth it.

Let's begin.

Day 1

Alcohol Island

I don't want to do this. Really, I don't. I don't want to admit that I need to change. I don't want to start this so-called "withdrawal process" or acknowledge—out loud—that things have spiraled out of control. I just want to fast-forward time. I want it to be two years from now when I'm fit, healthy, and free from alcohol.

But here I am. Stuck. I feel terrible.

So far today, I've eaten nothing but a miserable bacon sandwich and a bag of crisps. The sandwich tasted like it had been warmed up on a radiator, but I forced it down anyway, hoping it would soak up last night's alcohol. My size 42 jeans are digging into my stomach, my chest aches, and—like every single day—I'm absolutely exhausted.

I've gained over five stone in the last two years. When I catch a glimpse of myself in the mirror or see photos, I barely recognize the man staring back. When I run into people I haven't seen in years, they do a double take, struggling to place me. Some pat my stomach with a laugh and say, "How's it going, big man?" They mean no harm, but inside, it stings. I used to be 10 stone. I used to eat and drink whatever I wanted.

Now, I avoid certain people and social situations just to escape the embarrassment. But the worst part? I don't recognize myself, either. And I don't like the person I've become. It breaks my heart knowing that the last time my mum saw me before she passed, I was in this state.

Physically, I'm struggling. I can barely cut my toenails because my gut gets in the way. I wake up gasping for air, convinced I have sleep apnea. And every night, I repeat the same exhausting cycle—drinking until I crash, only to wake up dehydrated, sluggish, and full of regret.

I need to be clear—I'm not, and never have been, a heavy drinker. What I am is a consistent drinker. A mega-consistent drinker. Every single day, without fail, I drink.

A couple of pints of Kronenbourg at the local pub. A couple of bottles of Moretti at midnight when I get home. Every night, stealing hours from tomorrow just to drown out today. Wasting time. Wasting energy. Wasting my life.

But here's the thing—I've been here before, and I've climbed out of this pit before. And this time, I'm doing it differently. Writing It Down – For Me and You

Last time, I made it to Day 189 before I drank again. Believe it or not, it was easy. Yes, easy. But there's a catch. It only becomes easy after a week. Then, a month. Then two. By then, I didn't even think about alcohol. It was eliminated.

So why did I fall on Day 189? That story will come later. More importantly, I'll tell you the Golden Rules—the ones that have nothing to do with willpower and everything to do with breaking free for good.

But for now, this is Day 1. And if you're reading this, I'm guessing it's your Day 1, too. So, welcome. We're in this together.

Last Night, I had a dream about an argument at the pub over my January loyalty card—buy 10 pints, get 1 free. When I woke up, I ripped it up and threw it away at work. (Side note: it already had four stamps on it.)

I love my local. The Black Horse, It's a great place, full of fantastic people. And I don't judge anyone who enjoys a drink—I still am one of them. But for me? It's time.

I've been running on fumes for too long, and if I don't change now, I might never.

Let's do this.

Everyone has a Day 1. I'll tell you this for free, as they say in Yorkshire: Day 1 is the hardest, followed closely by Day 2. But after seven days, you'll feel elated. The first week is tough—not because you have to force yourself to avoid alcohol, but because you start feeling your emotions again. And that, more than anything, can be a shock to the system.

The reality is that alcohol has been numbing you. It's been dulling the edges of your emotions, turning life into a slightly blurry, slightly disconnected experience. When you remove it, everything sharpens. Your thoughts, your feelings, your memories—they all come back into focus. It can be overwhelming at first, but stick with it, and soon, you'll see it for what it truly is: freedom. The first few days will challenge you. Your mind will try to convince you that drinking is the solution when, in fact, it's been the problem all along. Stay with this feeling. Let it pass through you. You are stronger than you think.

So, what exactly is alcohol? Let's clear this up quickly. Alcohol—sometimes called ethanol—is the second most consumed psychoactive drug in the world, right behind caffeine. It's a central nervous system depressant, slowing down the electrical activity in your brain. The World Health Organization classifies it as toxic, psychoactive, dependence-producing, and even carcinogenic. Yet, somehow, we're conditioned to see it as a normal, even essential, part of life. From celebrations to commiserations, we are encouraged to drink. We toast with it, bond over it, and use it as a crutch when life gets difficult. But what if the very thing we turn to for relief is actually the source of our struggles?

The goal isn't to take it one day at a time while relying on sheer willpower to resist drinking. The goal is to reach a point where you can have a drink anytime you want but simply don't feel the need. A point where alcohol doesn't even cross your mind. If the thought of never drinking again fills you with fear, that's a clear sign it's time to begin. Day 1 is where it starts. And I promise, there is a world where alcohol is no longer part of your thought process.

This isn't about forcing yourself to quit. If you ever want a drink, you can have one. No one is stopping you. But before you do, give yourself a real shot at freedom by getting through the first seven days.

How bad is withdrawal, really? We're told it's nearly impossible, that we shouldn't even attempt it without medical intervention. The truth? It's weird. It can be uncomfortable. But it's absolutely doable. With the right approach, you can get through those first critical days and come out the other side stronger than ever. Day 7 is massive. If you can make it to Day 7, you can make it to Day 30. And if you can make it to Day

30, you'll start to experience something incredible—freedom. Alcohol will fade into the background, something you used to do but no longer care about. And when you look back, you'll ask yourself: "What the actual hell was I doing?"

Right now, you might not see it. But once you've put enough distance between yourself and alcohol, once you've rowed far enough away from that island, the view will change. You'll see it for what it really was. And when you do, you won't want to go back.

Each day without alcohol moves you 1,000 meters further from the island you don't yet realize you're trapped on. Keep going, and one day, it will disappear from view altogether.

Withdrawal is strange, sometimes unsettling, but also a powerful transformation. Embrace it. See it as proof that you're breaking free. Jason Vale once wrote: "The drug (alcohol) causes the need for the drug (alcohol)." Read that again. Understand it. Let it sink in. Because once you grasp this truth, everything starts to change.

Now, please do me a favor. Close your eyes and think of the happiest moment from your childhood. Maybe it was Christmas morning with your family, or riding your bike in the summer sun, or that holiday you'll never forget. Picture it clearly. Hear the sounds, feel the joy. Now ask yourself: Did alcohol play any part in that moment? Did you need alcohol to feel that happiness? Of course not. And you don't need it now. What you're about to gain—clarity, energy, deep and restorative sleep—will blow your mind.

I'm going to be completely honest in this book, sharing some of my deepest, darkest thoughts. Not just because it's therapeutic for me but because I know it will help others on this journey. This is Day 1, the hardest day. The next seven will be strange, but they won't be impossible.

Here's my plan to get through today—one I don't particularly want to follow, but I know I need to. At lunchtime, I'll go for a 30-minute walk, hoping to stand in some January sunlight. I'll listen to an audiobook by David Goggins (Can't Hurt Me) because his words remind me that I am capable of more than I think. Then, in the evening, I'll do something I hate: exercise. I'll drag my reluctant self into the garage and follow a dance workout called CIZE—not because I love it, but because it's fun enough to keep me moving. I'll do it at the time I'd normally be walking to the pub, replacing one habit with another. And if all goes well, I'll sleep better tonight than I have in years.

Speaking of sleep—this is where alcohol plays its nastiest tricks. The first few nights can be tough. You might lie there, wide awake, as your brain decides to replay every worst-case scenario and painful memory it can find. That's not you. That's the drug trying to reel you back in. Recognize it for what it is. Please don't fall for it. Instead, return to the happy moment you visualized earlier. If sleep doesn't come easily, just close your eyes and rest. Even lying awake, fully sober, is better than passing out with alcohol in your system. And if you really can't sleep, try this trick: tell yourself you'll stay awake all night. Next thing you know, you'll be out.

Maybe it'll be rough. Maybe it won't. Either way, you'll wake up tomorrow with Day 1 behind you. That's 1,000 meters further from Alcohol Island. One step closer to freedom. And that's all you need to focus on right now.

I'll be back tomorrow with Day 2. The hardest part will be behind us. You're not alone in this. You've got this book, and we've got each other. Keep going. You've got this.

Day 2

Full Swing

Well, I made it! Crashed into sleep like a ton of bricks last night—no tossing, no turning, just pure exhaustion after my lunchtime walk and that garage workout. Woke up feeling surprisingly positive, dragged myself into the shower, and shook off the morning fog a lot quicker than usual. The drive to work wasn't bad either. But as the hours tick by, the irritation is creeping in like an unwelcome guest. I knew this phase was coming, but that doesn't make it any less annoying. Every little thing is setting me off, and to top it off, I feel a little short of breath—probably from pushing myself too hard with the workout.

The biggest thing I've noticed today? Dehydration. My mouth feels like a desert, but for some weird reason, plain water isn't doing it for me. It's official—I've entered the cranky, irritable phase. The withdrawal is in full swing. It's funny how the body reacts when you suddenly cut out all the sugar, calories, and alcohol. This adjustment period is no joke, but I know it's just part of the process. My body is trying to recalibrate, and the tiredness is hitting like a truck.

This is a dangerous moment—the point where most people convince themselves that quitting is making them feel worse. The sneaky little voice whispers, "See? You felt fine when you were drinking." Lies. All lies. This is just the alcohol fighting for its place, trying to claw its way back in. Not a chance. Not today. I need to push through this. A sugary drink might help, maybe a nap if I can sneak one in later. Treating myself to something good to eat sounds like a solid plan too. But most importantly, I need to stay busy. Distraction is key—clean something, go for a walk, hit the shops, anything to fill the time I'd normally spend drinking. If I sit still, I'll overthink it, and that's a dangerous game.

10:17 AM. Do I want a drink? Absolutely not. This early in the day, alcohol isn't even on my radar. It's the evening that's the real battle. The habit, the routine—that's where the struggle lies. If you're in the same boat, be aware of your "regular time" and plan something to replace it. The mind plays tricks, making you think this withdrawal phase will last forever. It won't. Give it seven days, and you'll see.

The hardest part—Day 1—is behind me. Now, it's just a few days of this moodiness and exhaustion before I hit that golden moment. Around Day 7, something magical will happen. I know it because I've felt it before. It will come out of nowhere—maybe while I'm walking across the room, lying in bed, or just staring out the window—and suddenly, BAM! I'll feel good. Not just okay, but genuinely good. Lighter. Clearer. It's like stepping out of a fog and realizing you've been seeing the world through a dirty lens this whole time.

And then the best part—my brain will start wondering, "If I feel this good now, how much better could I actually feel?" That thought alone is enough to keep me going. I can't wait to write about it when it happens. But first, I have to get through these next few days.

12:09 PM. My imagination is going haywire. I feel lightheaded, almost like my brain is stuck between dreamland and reality. I need to clear my head. A lunchtime walk should help—fresh air, movement, a bit of a reset.

4:00 PM. What the hell is going on with my teeth? They ache, and a dull headache is settling in. My mood is absolute garbage right now. Everything and everyone is getting on my nerves. The office is unbearable, my thoughts are spiraling, and all I want is to go home and be alone. Tonight is going to be a test. I've got band rehearsal, and the hardest part won't be playing—it'll be what comes after. Walking out of that rehearsal room and not heading straight to the pub like I usually do. That moment will be my battlefield.

I'll check back in tomorrow with Day 2 in the bag. Probably.

Day 3

The Dream

Made it. But this was tough. I managed to go straight home after band rehearsal instead of wandering into the pub like I usually do. That alone felt like an impossible victory. The rush of playing music, the adrenaline, the high—it always makes a drink feel like the perfect encore. The pull was strong, but I resisted. Instead, I went home, threw together a late-night supper (a croissant with cheese—don't judge), and tried to unwind with an audiobook. The one I picked? The Unexpected Joy of Being Sober by Catherine Gray. It felt fitting. Intense. Maybe even a little ironic.

One thing I'll dive into later is the strategy of avoiding alcohol-heavy social situations in the first 7 to 30 days. It's crucial. At least for me, the temptation is too strong in the beginning. But after that period? I genuinely believe you can—and should—show up and enjoy those moments just as much, if not more, than before. I'll also get into ways to say no when people push drinks on you and why that moment of refusal can actually feel good. But for now, avoiding triggers is key.

Then came bedtime. And it was brutal.

It took me forever to fall asleep. This is that notorious 48-to-72-hour mark where alcohol does everything in its power to claw its way back into your system. It felt like my mind was playing tricks on me, whispering in the dark, trying to convince me to give in. Every time I drifted close to sleep, anxiety crept in. My brain ran worst-case scenarios on repeat, dragging me through every mistake, every regret, every haunting what-if. It was suffocating. I had to fight it—hard. I forced myself to think of my happy place, something peaceful, something that made me feel safe. Eventually, it worked. Sleep finally took over.

And then came the dream.

The moment I stop drinking, my dreams come back in full force. I've noticed this pattern before. It's almost as if my brain, no longer drowning in booze, suddenly unlocks another dimension. Usually, when I drink, the only time I dream is when my body jerks me awake at 3 a.m. for an emergency bathroom trip. But sober? My dreams are wild, vivid, and intense. My friends never believe me when I describe them, but I swear, this is exactly what happened in last night's dream:

I had a hospital appointment—something I'd dread in real life. When I arrived, I was told the consultant had bad news and that I needed to see him immediately. I walked into his office, but instead of a quiet, sterile room, I found myself standing in the middle of an arcade. The place was packed. Flashing lights, Space Invaders machines, the kind of electric buzz that makes you feel like you're trapped in an '80s movie. The noise was deafening, drowning out the consultant's words. I moved closer, straining to hear him. And then I saw him properly. My heart stopped.

It wasn't a doctor at all. It was my local pub landlord. The guy who's poured me countless pints, who's seen me at my best and my absolute worst. He was standing there in a long white coat, reading my medical results as if this was all perfectly normal. Before I could process what was happening, the scene shifted. Suddenly, I was on a tiny island in the middle of a lake—no bigger than a tennis court.

Someone told me I had two minutes to decide where I wanted to dig my grave. I couldn't choose. I turned around, and somehow, the grave was already dug. But it wasn't just a grave—it was enormous, almost like a pit, with rows of chairs lined up around it. Like an audience was expected.

And then my alarm went off. What a relief.

This is what alcohol does when it leaves your system. It fights. It twists your dreams, your thoughts, your cravings. It doesn't go quietly. Maybe the cheese croissant didn't help either. Who knows? But here I am, standing on the other side of Day Three, knowing deep down that this was a turning point. In a few days, it won't feel like this. The grip will loosen. The fog will lift. And already, despite the rough night, I feel... better.

I even feel rested, which is bizarre considering I didn't fall asleep until 2 a.m. Then again, I used to crash around the same time after a long night of drinking. But that wasn't real sleep. Alcohol ruins sleep in ways most people don't even realize. Sure, it might knock you out quickly, but it robs you of quality rest. It messes with REM sleep, leaving you restless and exhausted even after a full night in bed. And yet, when I drank, I convinced myself it helped me sleep. It never did.

My body still feels like it's catching up. I'm drinking more water than ever, yet I'm constantly thirsty. Which makes me wonder—just how dehydrated was I when I was drinking every day? The answer? Probably more than I want to admit.

But here's the thing: small wins matter. And last night, I caught one.

I was brushing my teeth, about to crash, when I caught my reflection in the mirror. Something was different. My face had a little more color. It wasn't much, but it was there—a small shift, a sign that my body was starting to recover. This morning, after my shower, my skin felt smoother and cleaner. No, I'm not morphing into Brad Pitt overnight, but I'll take it. A win is a win.

Now I'm deep into Day Three, and something has changed. I have something I didn't have on Day One: momentum. It's building. I can feel it. To quit now would mean wasting three whole days of work, and I'm not about to do that. In a week, I'll be stronger. In a month, I'll be thriving. The time will pass no matter what—I might as well make it count.

And you know what? Writing this is helping. A lot. It feels like I'm writing myself sober, shaping my own story as I go. Maybe you should try it too. Maybe this is part of the process. Find whatever works. Keep going.

Day 4

Bullseye

Made it to day 4, Thursday. Last night was a quiet one, just me in the garage playing darts. It felt good to keep myself occupied, and I had already made up my mind that I wasn't going to the pub. There was no internal debate, no back-and-forth bargaining with myself. That decision had been made earlier, and I stuck to it. Maybe that's the trick—removing the question altogether instead of trying to argue with my own cravings. It seemed to work because I didn't feel deprived or restless. I just got on with my night, and it passed without much of a struggle.

Sleep came easily. I got my 10,000 steps in during the day, which probably helped tire me out. The strangest thing, though, was the dream I had. I found myself in a pub, meeting my family for Sunday lunch, but for some reason, I had ordered a pint of bitter. Before I could even drink it, I fell asleep at the table, and when my family arrived, they just left me there in the corner, sleeping. When I woke up, I had that moment of panic—did I actually drink? But no, it was just a dream. A weird one, but harmless. Aside from that, the night was fine, no real tossing and turning, no waking up in a sweat. Just sleep. Real, restful sleep. I woke up feeling like I had actually rested. For the first time in a long time, I didn't feel completely drained in the morning.

I had a dull headache when I got up, but nothing too bad. It didn't feel like the dehydration headaches I used to get from drinking, more like a residual tension headache, the kind that lingers as your body adjusts. Despite that, I felt surprisingly positive for a cold, dark January morning. And here's something I wasn't expecting—I actually caught myself singing along to the radio on my way to work. That's not something I'd normally do, especially not before a cup of Yorkshire tea. But there I was, singing along, and I had this fleeting moment of realization: maybe I'm starting to feel a little better. Maybe there's something to this after all.

Exercise has been a huge help, even if I don't always enjoy it. Yesterday, I did a quick ten-minute walk before work and another thirty minutes at lunch. That, plus some dart-throwing in the garage, pushed me over the 10,000-step mark. It's not a miracle cure, but it does help. Walking is one of those things that almost anyone can do, and it clears my head. The fresh air, the movement—it all seems to take the edge off, especially in the evenings when cravings tend to creep in. And if nothing else, it makes me tired enough to sleep.

This morning, standing in the shower, I noticed something—just a little, but enough. My reflection looked a bit less bloated and a bit less swollen. Not a dramatic change, but enough to make me pause. Right now, I'm still in the shape of Tony Green from from the 80's TV show Bullseye, but at least I'm moving in the right direction. Weight loss isn't my primary focus yet; that will come naturally as the drinking stops and the calories drop. One thing at a time. First, I need to rebuild my habits, my routines, and my mindset. The physical changes will follow in time.

Momentum is powerful. Each day that passes builds on the last. The more I push through, the easier it becomes to keep going. I know that right now, some people might be reading this and thinking, No way. I'm too tired for exercise. I can barely function. But I promise, it helps. It doesn't have to be a hardcore workout. Just movement. Just fresh air. It clears your mind, resets your body, and makes sleeping easier. It's a cycle that feeds itself—the more I do, the better I feel, and the better I feel, the more I want to do.

I caught myself wondering about goals today. Not just short-term ones but long-term ones. I'd love to make it a full year without drinking. That thought alone feels massive, almost too big to process, I'd also love to get down to 12 stone 7. It's been years since I've been at that weight. But more than anything, I just want someone to notice. I want someone to look at me and say, you're looking good. You look healthier. I don't even care about the number on the scale as much as I care about that validation, that moment when the effort starts to show.

There's one weird thing I've noticed—sweating. A lot. Under my arms, mostly, but just generally feeling hotter than usual. I said I'd document everything, so here it is: I'm sweating more than normal, and I don't know why. Maybe my body is finally catching up, processing everything that's been sitting in my system for years. Maybe it's flushing things out. Or maybe it's just my body adjusting to the change. Either way, I'll take it as a positive. It means something is shifting.

Four days down. Four days of no alcohol. Four nights of proper sleep. Four mornings where I haven't woken up feeling like a failure. It's a small number, but it's growing. Every day that passes is one more that I don't have to relive the regret, one more step away from the person I don't want to be anymore.

I don't know what tomorrow will bring, but I know this: I won't drink today. And that's enough.

Day 5

Bert

Today was brutal. I spent the entire day on my feet, unboxing items in a stiflingly hot room, sweat pooling, exhaustion gnawing at my patience. Somewhere in the chaos, a voice crept into my head. "After all this, you deserve a cold beer later." It lingered, whispering doubts. "How on earth are you going to manage without a beer for the rest of your life anyway?" It was relentless, digging away at me, trying to find a crack in my resolve.

I've decided that this voice needs a name. Something to separate it from me, to make it something I can ignore, dismiss, even ridicule. I'll call it Bert. Next time Bert shows up, I'll recognize him instantly. I'll picture the Sesame Street puppet of the same name, stuff him back into his crate, and nail the lid shut. "That's just Bert. Bye, Bert." Odd? Maybe. But if it works, it works.

Bedtime was the worst yet. The hot flushes hit hard, followed by this cycle of falling asleep only to jolt awake in panic. Every time I closed my eyes, something yanked me back to consciousness. It took hours to settle, but when I finally did, I slept deeply. No nightmares. No interruptions. Just sleep. I woke up feeling like I had actually rested, something I hadn't experienced in a long time. My thirst is still relentless, but there's a strange satisfaction in knowing that I'm no longer ruining my body with alcohol every night. Four nights of sober sleep. That's something worth holding onto.

What's really striking me now is how much better I feel in the mornings. The self-loathing isn't as suffocating. I don't wake up hating myself for wasting yet another night drinking. I'm not dragging myself through the day drained and embarrassed. I'm actually getting things done—at work, at home. I'm present. And I'm realizing that those few hours I used to spend drinking, mindlessly staying up until 1 AM, weren't worth sacrificing the entire next day for. That's where the real exhaustion came from. It wasn't just the alcohol; it was the lost time, the wasted energy. I used to be so drained that I'd sneak off to my car during lunch breaks just to nap for 30 minutes, desperate to make it through the afternoon. That's not normal. That's not okay.

Science says the alcohol is out of my system now. But the real challenge isn't physical—it's mental. It's the habits, the associations, the way alcohol has woven itself into my routine. Tonight, for example, I've got band rehearsal. My brain automatically follows the pattern: band rehearsal, then beer. It's been my ritual for months, maybe years. Breaking that connection isn't instant. It's a slow process, a rewiring that takes time. But one day, I'll leave rehearsal, head home, and realize I never even thought about drinking. That's the goal. That's the turning point.

And then there's moderation. The biggest trap of all. The moment you think you've got control, that you're free, that's when the voice—Bert—gets clever. "You're fine now. You've beaten this. You can have just one." It's the most dangerous lie. I know this because I've fallen for it before.

I made it 189 days sober once. And after the first few weeks, it wasn't a fight. It wasn't a struggle. It wasn't even a thought. Alcohol just wasn't a part of my life anymore. No cravings. No bad dreams. No sense in missing out. Just normalcy. A clean, sober, uncomplicated life. And then, one day, Bert got to me.

It was November. I hate November. The darkness, the cold, the damp, the way it suffocates me. I live for summer—the long days, the smell of fresh-cut grass, the warmth on my skin. But in November, all of that disappears, and so does my motivation. My depression creeps in. I hate Halloween. I hate fireworks. I hate the fog. That's when Bert saw his chance.

Day 189. I spent the entire day ripping up and replacing bathroom floorboards, backbreaking, exhausting work. And all day, Bert was there. "You deserve a drink after this. One drink. Just one." I told myself I had it under control. "Six months sober. That's enough, right? I've proven my point." That night, I walked to the pub, convincing myself it was just a one-off. Just a couple of beers, just to remind myself why I don't drink anymore.

I remember that first pint. It was disappointing and underwhelming. No magic. No relief. So, I had another. And another. And by the time I got home, I cracked open a few more bottles. And just like that, moderation won. and then… 443 days of drinking. Not a single break.

That's the trap of moderation. It doesn't start with a drinking problem; it starts with a thinking problem. Bert isn't the alcohol. Bert is the thought process that makes you think you can handle alcohol. And this time around, Bert isn't winning.

I'm working on a plan to make sure of it. More on that later. But for now, moderation is off the table.

Speaking of struggles, I had a hell of a moment today. Went for a walk, bundled up in layers because it's January, and ended up overheating like an idiot. Seventeen stone of alcohol weight and a sudden drop in sugar levels did not mix well. By the time

I got back to work, I felt like I was going to pass out. Had to sneak into a toilet cubicle, strip off my coat, jumper, and t-shirt, and just sit there, sweating and gasping like a broken radiator. It was pathetic. I felt like a complete mess, a big, overheated, bloated wreck. Ended up dragging myself to the canteen and grabbing a Yorkie and a full-fat Coke just to stabilize. It was scary.

But you know what? It was also a wake-up call. My body is in shock from all this change. Years of drinking, abusing my health, stuffing myself with sugar and alcohol—this is the fallout. And it just proves that I'm doing the right thing. My body is screaming for help, and for the first time in a long time, I'm actually listening.

Is it too late? No. It's never too late. I've made it to day five. And I'm not stopping n

Day 6 - 7

Peugeot.

Friday night tested my resolve. After band rehearsal, Bert was at it again, trying to lure me into the pub. "Just one on a Friday," he said. "Make it the only night you go out. That's not too bad, right? You can moderate."

It was tempting, the way he made it sound so reasonable. But I didn't go. I made it home, and the urge passed. I felt good about that. Until Saturday night rolled around. And there it was again, the same old argument: "Come on, it's Saturday! It's the weekend; surely you can go out on a Saturday?" It was almost comical how predictable the thoughts were. And yet, even though I could anticipate them, they still tried to wear me down. I've noticed the cravings are strongest between nine and ten at night. That's the window when the pull of routine tries to drag me back into old habits. But once again, I held my ground.

Saturday was particularly hard. It would have been my mum's birthday, only the second one since she passed away. Grief has a way of sneaking up when you least expect it, and I could feel its weight pressing down on me all day. But I kept myself busy. I had been working on a small, battered old Peugeot 206 car—21 years old, to be exact—and I took it in for its MOT. It passed. That felt like a little victory. Later in the afternoon, I visited my dad, spent some time with him, and then came back home and polished the car before putting it up for sale. By the time the evening came, I was exhausted. Physically drained from the day's work, mentally worn from the emotions that had been simmering beneath the surface. But I made it through. That was Day Six, done.

Day Seven greeted me with the luxury of a lie-in. The dreams are becoming less strange, and sleep is coming more naturally. That's progress. I know I should be proud of myself for making it this far, and I am, but I refuse to get ahead of myself. Until I wake up on Day Eight, Day Seven isn't officially over. No celebrating before the job is done.

I spent some time yesterday thinking about Bert—my inner demon voice, the one that whispers temptations in my ear. I decided he needed a nemesis, someone to shut him up when he started rattling his cage. And then it hit me. That someone is me. It's my voice that needs to be louder. My will that needs to be stronger. I'm taking back control. Bert doesn't get to call the shots anymore.

This week has been one of the most productive I've had in a long time. Sure, there have been wobbles, but I've kept going. And that's the real victory. I can feel my confidence creeping back in and see the slight deflation of my bloated face in the mirror. It's not drastic, but it's something. And something is better than nothing.

I've been watching stories of celebrities who have quit drinking—something about hearing their experiences makes me feel less alone in this. Dick Van Dyke, still going strong at 99, once battled alcohol. Anthony Hopkins, too, has spoken openly about his struggles. Their stories are motivating. They made it through, and so can I. I can feel things changing in small but noticeable ways. My senses are sharper; I can see better, smell better. The fog that used to cloud my mind is starting to lift, and for 23 hours of the day, I barely even think about alcohol. It's just that one stubborn hour—between nine and ten at night—that still tries to trip me up. But I'm learning to navigate it. Keeping busy helps. And when all else fails, I just go to bed early. Because if I wake up sober, I win.

Mornings have become my favorite part of the day. That's when the real benefits shine through. I wake up without that heavy, aching sick feeling behind my eyes. My chest isn't burning with heartburn. I actually feel hungry, and not for greasy, regret-filled meals, but for real food. Good food. My body is adjusting, repairing itself, and I can feel it happening.

Day Eight is on the horizon, and for the first time in a long time, I'm looking forward to it.

One of the funniest moments of the weekend was when my wife made a joke about bin day. "Next week," she said, "there will only be a single glass jam jar in the recycling bin. The bin men will probably think you've moved out." I laughed because she wasn't wrong. Usually, I'd be lugging down 60 empty beer bottles, looking like a contestant in some budget version of "World's Strongest Man." Not this time.

I feel like I'm sailing away from Alcohol Island. The first week felt like battling through choppy waters, fighting against the waves, but I've made it past that first rough stretch. Now, it's calmer.

Not easy, but manageable. I could look back at the island and see where I was, and for the first time, I could recognize just how ridiculous my drinking habits had become. It's sobering—pun intended—but it's also empowering. I don't have to live that way anymore. I'm choosing something better.

The next challenge is getting back to a weight that feels right. My goal is twelve stone seven. That's where I was before alcohol became a regular, unwelcome guest in my life. Getting back there will take time, but I've done the crime, so now I need to do the time. One step at a time.

Now, it's time for bed. When I wake up, I'll be on Day Eight. And that's something worth looking forward to.

Day 8

Bananaman

Day 7 is finally behind me, and I wake up to the morning of Day 8 feeling like a different person from the one who started this journey just a week ago. I went back and read my Day 1 entry, and the difference is staggering. I feel a thousand times better—lighter, clearer, more in control. I deserve a reward, and I'll make sure to treat myself to something later. There's still a long way to go, but for the first time in a while, I don't feel like a complete embarrassment to myself. My energy is slowly coming back, though my body still seems confused, adjusting to this sudden change. Seven days in, and one question keeps circling my mind: Am I an alcoholic?

I keep thinking about something I read in Jason Vale's book, **Kick** the Drink Easily. He poses a question that really stuck with me: Are you a bananaholic? It sounds ridiculous, but that's exactly the point. If I ate a can of baked beans every day, would that make me a baked-bean-aholic? No one gets labeled a "bananaholic" for eating too many bananas. And yet, when it comes to alcohol, society has created this word—alcoholic—as if it's some special kind of affliction, separate from any other addiction. But alcohol is a drug, just like heroin, cocaine, or nicotine. We call people addicted to those substances drug addicts, so why not alcohol? Why not just call it what it is? A dependency. A habit. An addiction.

The alcohol industry and the media have done a fantastic job convincing the world that alcohol is a different kind of drug—one that's normal to consume, and abnormal to avoid. It's the only drug where people question you for not taking it. No one ever asks, "Hey, what's wrong with you? You haven't done heroin today." But turn down a drink at the pub, and suddenly, you're the one with the problem. Society makes it seem like quitting alcohol is nearly impossible, that if you do manage to quit, you must have some deep, underlying issue. But that's just another illusion created to keep people drinking. The truth is, quitting is absolutely possible. People do it all the time. And I'm doing it right now.

Even though I reject the label of alcoholic, I still take full responsibility for my situation. I don't smoke—I never have—but I imagine that if I started, within a couple of months, I'd be hooked. The same principle applies to alcohol. I opened that box, and once it was open, the habit took root. Now, I have to pay the price for my past choices. If I had never started drinking, I wouldn't be here now, working to undo the damage. I fully believe that because I allowed alcohol into my life, I will always have some kind of craving, no matter how small. But how small can I make it? A year from now, will I still be thinking about pints at the local pub every night? How much of my mind will alcohol still occupy? I bet I can get it down to five or ten percent, and the further I get from my last drink, the weaker that craving will become.

This is why I don't subscribe to the whole one-day-at-a-time mentality. I refuse to live as if I'm constantly depriving myself of something. I'm not missing out—I'm breaking free. The only reason I ever craved alcohol was because alcohol itself created that craving. Now that it's out of my system, it's over. My body isn't asking for it anymore. It's only my mind—my old patterns, my old habits—that try to pull me back in. That's where Bert comes in.

Bert is my inner demon, the voice in my head that whispers, "Go on, just one. It's the weekend. You deserve it." He used to have control over me, but I see him for what he is now. And every day, he gets weaker. His tricks are old news. I recognize them the moment they appear, and I shut him down before he can get a word in. He's consuming less of my thoughts, and I can feel myself breaking free. It might sound strange, but this way of thinking works for me. It gives me something tangible to fight against.

The next step is hitting thirty days and strengthening my mindset. I also need to figure out how to patch the hole where I slipped up last time. I made it to Day 189 before, and look back at the island. This time, I need a plan for when that moment comes. The truth is, the urge to drink doesn't just appear out of nowhere—it starts building days, even weeks before the actual relapse happens. I've noticed that when I've gone months without drinking, Bert starts creeping back in, planting little thoughts in my mind long before I actually pick up a drink. This is where I've failed before.

I need to prepare for that moment now while I'm still strong. I need something in place—a safety net, a person to talk to, a strategy for when the old thoughts start sneaking in. I won't let history repeat itself. More on that later, though. For now, I've made it to Day 8, and that's something to be proud of. The first seven days were brutal, but they're done. The hardest part is behind me.

Day 9

Aiwa

Last night felt like the most "normal" night I've had in a long time. The thought of going out for a pint didn't even cross my mind until around 10:15 PM, and when it did, the urge was fleeting. I fought it off with ease and went to bed instead, exhausted from the day. Between my lunchtime walk, an evening workout DVD, and a game of darts in the garage, I had worn myself out completely.

Not drinking hasn't been as hard as it was in the first few days. The cravings don't hit as often, and when they do, they pass quicker. But one thing remains constant—I wake up every morning feeling incredibly thirsty. It's like my body is still adjusting, purging itself of something it had depended on for too long. And just like last Tuesday, after a day of exercise, I woke up completely out of breath. It's unsettling. I have a doctor's appointment on Thursday, and I'm planning to bring up the possibility of sleep apnea. I haven't woken up gasping for air recently, but I often feel like something heavy has been pressing down on my chest all night. My kids have even come into the bedroom at night to ask me to stop snoring. It's that bad.

I've tried all sorts of devices—the nasal strips, the sprays—none of them work. I considered a mouth guard, but my gag reflex makes that impossible. What a state to be in, really. It's frustrating to realize that something as simple as breathing at night has become a struggle, and I can't help but think my weight gain from years of drinking has played a massive role in this. It's a vicious cycle—alcohol leads to weight gain, weight gain worsens sleep apnea, and poor sleep makes it harder to lose weight. I read a brilliant book called "The Gabriel Method" by Jon Gabriel, where he emphasizes how crucial it is to address sleep apnea before even attempting to lose weight. It makes so much sense. Looking at his before and after photos is proof enough that real change is possible.

Lately, I've been thinking a lot about how my relationship with alcohol began. My childhood home was practically alcohol-free. My parents didn't drink at all, except for a small glass of wine on Christmas Day when relatives visited. That was it. There was never any talk about alcohol, never any exposure to it in our home life. So, when did it start? I suppose it began in my teenage years. One of my friends' dads worked at John Smith's brewery, which meant we had easy access to "discounted" cans. My mum eventually found an entire crate of Carling Premier under my bed. She was furious. She asked if I had a drinking problem, and I just laughed. To me, it was ridiculous. I wasn't drinking every night or getting into trouble. It was just a bit of fun, right? She wasn't laughing, though.

Back then, it wasn't an issue. I could take it or leave it. But I did have this habit—I'd sit on my bedroom floor at night with my AIWA CD player and a massive pair of over-ear headphones, listening to music and sipping on a can of Carling Premier. It felt like the perfect way to unwind. I can't lie; it felt amazing. But that feeling, that buzz, it fades over time. And before you know it, you're no longer drinking for pleasure. You're drinking because you have to.

My mum warned me. She told me that if I drank enough, I'd reach a point where I wouldn't be able to stop. I dismissed her immediately. That would never happen to me. No way. But she was right. They usually are, aren't they?

At the time, I had phases where I drank, but it never felt like a problem. That all changed when I moved into my first home. I had an alcoholic neighbor who went out drinking every single night. I used to think, "What a loser." The irony isn't lost on me now. He'd come home at 1 or 2 AM, slamming doors, playing loud music, making a racket. The problem was that I worked shifts. I had to be up at 5 AM. Sleep became impossible. And then, one night, I figured out a solution—

alcohol. If I drank enough, I wouldn't care about the noise. A few cans, some earplugs, and I was out cold. It worked. Too well.

The habit escalated from there. At first, it was just a few nights a week. Then, it was every night. The more I drank, the more normal it felt. The routine became embedded in my life. Then came the gambling. I joined an online betting site called Profit Maximiser, which allowed me to cash out bonus offers by laying bets off at an exchange. It was brilliant at first. I made nearly 3K. But instead of saving it, investing it, or doing something useful with it—I treated myself. I started going to the pub regularly. No more cans at home; now I had the real thing. And that's how the habit of popping down to my local was born.

The problem? My local is fantastic. Too good. I've often joked that I wish it would shut down because, honestly, none of the other pubs in the village have the same pull. The camaraderie, the atmosphere, the familiarity—it's intoxicating, even without the alcohol. Slowly, my casual habit turned into a daily one. And once that switch flips, it's hard to turn it back. The drug creates the need for the drug.

Now, on day nine of sobriety, I can see it all so clearly. The buzz I used to chase? It's gone. It's been gone for a long time. What's left is just a time-consuming, money-draining cycle that exists to feed itself. The need to drink to put out the flames of the previous drink, and then again, and again. A never-ending loop. It creeps up on you, just like it did with me. And if I'm being completely honest, it nearly killed me. Maybe it still will. Not through alcohol poisoning, but through everything that comes with it—weight gain, depression, the slow erosion of self-worth. I'm only on day nine, but I can already see how much of my life alcohol has stolen from me.

Yet, there's hope. I can feel it. I'm waiting for that "Aha!" moment, the one where everything just clicks, and I suddenly realize I don't need alcohol anymore. I'm not quite there yet, but I know I'm moving in the right direction. The island of alcohol that once felt like home is getting smaller in the distance. I'm relieved to be **rowing** away from it. I have no desire to go back.

Tomorrow marks double digits. Day ten. That feels like something worth celebrating. Not with a drink, of course, but maybe with something that actually brings me joy. This afternoon, I'm going to start looking for an accountability group—someone I can call when the urge hits, someone who can remind me why I'm doing this. Because I never want to have another day one.

Day 10

Wonka

Double figures today. It feels like I'm starting to settle into this like the struggle is easing up. Last night, as usual, temptation showed up right after my band rehearsal—that familiar pull, like an old friend who only brings trouble. As mentioned, I've started calling and visualizing as Bert from Sesame Street, as if naming it makes it easier to handle. Adrenaline is definitely a trigger for me. That post-rehearsal rush used to send me straight to the pub, but last night, for the first time, I didn't even entertain the idea. No internal debate, no back-and-forth. I just went home, had some supper, watched a bit of TV, and went to bed. Simple. Easy. Right.

Sleep came without resistance. No restless tossing and turning, no bad dreams, no waking up choking on my breath. It's a strange thing to notice, but it hit me this morning—how much easier it is just to exist now. The absence of discomfort is something I had long forgotten.

I thought about it for a second—what's best for me? Dragging myself home in the early hours after a couple of pints, drinking lager until 2 AM, and then struggling through an exhausting next day? Or this? A quiet night, restful sleep, and waking up feeling human? The choice is so clear now.

I caught my reflection in the mirror and noticed something—I don't look as grey anymore. There's actual color in my face, and my jeans feel a little looser. Maybe they've just stretched out from a few days of wear, but I'd like to believe it's something more. The bloatedness is fading, and for the first time in ages, I feel like I have a shot at getting back in shape. It's funny how quickly the body starts responding when you stop poisoning it.

It's easy, though, when you start feeling better, to forget just how bad it was. That's why I think it's important to write it all down—the daily struggles, the things I tolerated for years as if they were normal. Not just a pros-and-cons list of drinking, but an actual record of what it did to me.

Tiredness. Low self-esteem. Heartburn. Dull headaches. Constant lethargy. A hunger that never actually felt like hunger, just an empty, desperate need to consume something. Thirst that no amount of water could quench. The frustration of feeling tied to alcohol's schedule, planning everything around when I could drink. Weight gain. Bad breath. Bags under my eyes. Spending over a hundred pounds a week on this habit. I woke up in the middle of the night; my bladder was about to explode. Terrible sleep quality. Overthinking everything, constant brain fog. Sore, bloodshot eyes. Snoring so badly I'd wake up gasping. Almost fell asleep at work. Dozing off in my car at lunchtime just to function.

The worst part? The loss of hope. The slow erosion of confidence. The creeping belief that there was no future for me. That's the real damage alcohol did. The list could go on forever, but just writing it down makes it clear—this wasn't just "a few drinks." It was a problem. Not in the way society labels alcoholics but in the way that I had willingly built my life around a drug, the most widely accepted one of all.

But today, Day 10, I feel something I haven't felt in a long time—optimism. It's fragile, a tiny spark, but it's there. I keep wondering where this path might take me. How good can life actually get if I keep going? It's been so long since I've thought like this.

This morning, I heard a song from the new Wonka movie—"For a Moment." The lyrics hit me hard:

"For a moment, life doesn't seem quite so bad,

For a moment, I kind of forgot to be sad."

That's me today. For a moment, I forgot to be sad. I also stumbled upon another song recently from Cobra Kai called "Back in the Game." A completely different energy from Wonka, but it spoke to me just the same:

"I'm back in the game,

Breaking hearts again.

You better watch out,

"Cause I'm back in the game."

That's how I feel right now. Back in the game. Back in society. Like I'm waking up after being asleep for years. It's hard to describe, but for the first time in a long time, I feel like I have a chance. Mental clarity is creeping in. The sun is shining today for the first time in months, and that definitely helps.

Looking back at that list of symptoms, the difference between then and now is like night and day. I can't believe I lived that way for so long, convincing myself it was fine. I've been consuming as much positivity as possible—avoiding the news and dodging Facebook doom-scrolling. I don't need to be weighed down by the world's problems when I'm just starting to lift my burdens. Instead, I've flipped the script.

Tony Robbins, Mel Robbins, David Goggins, Paul McKenna—these voices are filling my head instead of the usual self-doubt. I've been watching sobriety stories on YouTube, listening to motivational music, and feeding my mind with anything that keeps me moving forward.

Here's a little trick I've found—watching something that makes you feel alive. For me, it's Michael Jackson. Always has been. Seeing him move, that effortless precision, that raw energy—it never fails to light me up. The Motown 25 reunion performance? Perfection. For you, it might be something different. Arnold Schwarzenegger, an epic NFL comeback, the greatest tiddlywinks shot of all time—whatever it is, watch it daily. Let it remind you that it's okay to feel excited, to feel inspired, to feel good. It might have been a while since you let yourself feel that way.

Alcohol is a central nervous system depressant—it literally slows down the brain. But it's out of my system now. I'm not numbed anymore. I'm in control. I can feel happiness, even if it's just for a moment. And I can build on that.

Looking back at alcohol from here, it's so obvious—what a trap it was. A depressing, time-consuming, money-sucking trap. A cycle of false highs and permanent lows. A relentless craving, always leading back to the same place. But today, I'm further away from that island. I can see it for what it really is. And I don't ever want to go back.

Today is Day 10. From here, I start looking forward. I start taking full control. The future isn't just something I endure anymore—it's something I get to create.

Day 11 - 15

Honeymoon

Two weeks sober now, and life is starting to feel a little easier. I can sense my confidence creeping back in small, unexpected ways. There are still mood swings—one moment, I'm driving to work, marveling at the frozen landscape, the trees standing still as if suspended in time, and instead of cursing the winter cold, I find myself thinking, What a wonderful world. But then, later in the day, I catch myself being short with someone, my patience wearing thin over something trivial. The emotional rollercoaster is still there, but at least I'm aware of it now.

Physically, I can already see changes. I've lost a couple of pounds, something I haven't managed to do in ages. The walking and exercise DVDs are starting to pay off. The best part, though, is that I seem to have moved past that crushing anxiety—the desperate, all-consuming need to drink just to keep the flames of alcohol withdrawal at bay. That moment in the day when I would crave a pint when my mind would be solely focused on that first sip, has loosened its grip on me. My bank account is also starting to breathe a sigh of relief. It's shocking to realize just how much money I was pouring into alcohol without a second thought.

A few days ago, I got an offer from Apple Music—three months for £10.99. My initial reaction? No way! But later, it hit me: I used to spend that amount daily in the pub without even questioning it. That realization hit like a ton of bricks. Alcohol had been draining my finances, yet I never batted an eye. It was absolute madness. When you're caught in the cycle, you don't see it. You just keep running on the treadmill, blind to how much you're giving up. As a small celebration, I took the Apple Music offer—though, truth be told, I'm still more of a CD guy.

Since leaving Alcohol Island, I've found myself doing so much more. It's not just the hours I spent in the pub—it's the time before and after, the lethargy, the mind fog, the exhaustion. Now, I have bags of energy. My creativity has ignited in ways I never expected. In the last two weeks, I bought, repaired, and sold a car for profit—something I used to love doing. It reminded me of my old YouTube channel, Repairing Lawnmowers for Profit. I haven't uploaded in a while, but maybe it's time to get back to it. I've also been learning how to publish books online and even published a cat word search.

But the best part? I've been more present with my kids. We've been fixing things around the house, playing darts, and even repairing the car together. This past weekend, we went into the city for a game of snooker. It might not sound like much, but when I was drinking, I never had the energy. I was constantly drained, just going through the motions. Now, I can be bothered. And honestly? I've barely thought about alcohol at all. That's a great sign. But I know there will be tests ahead.

Sleep has been incredible. There's no greater joy than getting into bed completely sober, pulling the covers up, resting my head on the pillow, and knowing I'll get a full, uninterrupted 7-8 hours of proper sleep. I can't even put into words how good that feels. There's an MP3 download online by Jon Gabriel called Evening Visualization. It's meant for weight loss, but it helps me wind down and fall asleep effortlessly. I haven't struggled with sleep or had bad dreams in over a week, though I did have a persistent headache all weekend. Thankfully, it's gone now.

You might think it's all smooth sailing from here—that I've cracked the code, and life is sunshine and roses now that I've broken free from alcohol's grip. Not quite. This, I realize, is the honeymoon phase. And like every honeymoon, it won't last. Normality, strangely enough, is a trigger. At first, you're riding the high of making it through the hardest part, patting yourself on the back. But then, life just… becomes normal again. And in that normalcy, it's easy to let your guard down.

To start romanticizing moderation. To become less busy. And when life throws its inevitable stressors at you, the temptation to drink can reappear from nowhere.

I like to think of it as Snakes and Ladders. The more days you put between yourself and alcohol, the better. But there will always be snakes—always a chance to slide back down. And if you do, you wake up back on Alcohol Island. Day one. Again. And we don't want that.

The next phase is about true freedom. It's about putting steps in place to ensure I don't make a reckless decision that lands me back where I started. One thing that helps is reminding myself that I can drink whenever I want—I'm just choosing not to. This isn't about willpower. It's about common sense. No one can make me drink. The only way alcohol enters my body is if I decide to pick up a drink and pour it down my throat. And I won't.

For some, the "one day at a time" approach works. I have no experience with Alcoholics Anonymous, but I imagine that's their philosophy. And if that works for you, fantastic. Keep going. But for me, that mindset doesn't work. One day at a time feels like abstaining, like I'm depriving myself of something pleasurable. But I'm not. I don't have alcohol in my system. I'm not "going without" alcohol any more than I'm going without baked beans. Different approaches work for different people. This one works for me.

I know this might sound like it's all been easy for me like I just decided to quit, and suddenly, my life transformed. But it wasn't easy at first. The truth is, it is easy now—shockingly easy, just 15 days in. And if you're reading this, hesitating to start, let me tell you exactly what you're thinking. It's easy for you, but I drink more than you do. My situation is different.

Let me remind you: I drank for 443 consecutive days.

If the thought of stopping terrifies you, your brain will find every excuse to put it off. You'll tell yourself you'll start on Monday. Or after the wedding. Or whenever. But if you know deep down that you need to take back control, start today. Make today your Day One. Who knows where your sober adventure will take you a year from now?

I'm genuinely excited to see what a full year of sobriety looks like. To be fully awake, fully aware, not trapped in a cycle of exhaustion and self-loathing. One thing I do each day is take a photo of myself. I know it sounds weird, but I did it last time for 189 days. It's amazing to see the gradual transformation—the clearer skin, the healthier face, the brighter eyes. It's a powerful motivator.

Today, a friend from my local pub messaged me to check in. A good friend—someone I've spent countless hours with over the years. I won't lie, I miss the social aspect of the pub a little. But in time, I'll find new ways to socialize. The strange thing is, not drinking **Whilst** in a pub is actually an incredibly enjoyable experience. In 2025, saying no to alcohol isn't difficult. It's becoming more and more normal. In the coming pages, I'll talk more about this, about how not drinking can be one of the most liberating choices you ever make.

At the end of the day, it's just a small change. But it improves every aspect of your life. And that, in itself, makes it worth it.

Day 16

Jog on

Day 16 started with a jolt—almost quite literally. I nearly ran over a jogger in my car. Not even joking. I was turning left into the estate where I work, indicators on, lights on, everything done by the book. And then, out of nowhere, this jogger—probably too focused on shaving a few seconds off his best Strava time—decided to dash straight across the road. It was like a scene out of Trainspotting, that moment when Renton collides with a car while running from the police. Only this time, my jogger stopped just in time. His face, a mix of sheer panic and relief, said it all. I just kept driving, resisting the urge to shake my head in disbelief.

But as I continued on, a thought hit me—what if I had been drinking last night? Not blackout drunk, just my usual routine: a couple of pints, a few bottles. Would I have stopped in time? Or would I have ploughed into him? The terrifying part is, I never actually considered myself a drink driver before. But had I been? Even if I had been under the legal limit, alcohol slows reaction times. Maybe last night's drinks wouldn't have mattered. Maybe they would have. The unsettling part is, you don't get a do-over to find out.

I always make sure to arrive fifteen minutes early for work, taking a quiet walk from 7:45 to 8:00 AM. It's my little strategy to avoid the stress of heavier traffic. I drive carefully, I think more clearly. Maybe that habit alone saved the jogger today. But what if things had played out differently? If I had hit him, the news headline would have read: 55-year-old charity runner killed by suspected drunk driver. That label would stick forever. His family would be left shattered, and I'd be the man responsible for taking a life.

As dramatic as it sounds, the whole thing shook me. He must have been around sixty, but he was absolutely flying down that road. And I'd bet anything he was glued to his fitness tracker, focused on the data rather than reality. His Strava route nearly led him straight to the morgue.

The encounter left my mind spinning—about the past, the present, and the future. I keep coming back to this thought: life without alcohol versus life as an addict. What will it really look like? The answer is becoming clearer. Without alcohol, I have a future. I'm not just dragging myself through the motions, exhausted and detached. I had my first aha! moment today, and it hit me in the simplest way. As I walked before work, something felt different. Lighter. Easier. At first, I thought it was because I wasn't carrying my rucksack. Then I realized—I never walk with my rucksack. It wasn't my load that had changed. It was me. I felt lighter and stronger. Maybe the first signs of fitness are returning. Maybe fifteen nights of quality sleep working their magic.

Evenings are the hardest part now. Before, they were my sanctuary. My time. The pub, the drinks, the Netflix marathons till 2 AM. My reward for making it through the day. Now, I see those hours for what they were—ruining the next day before it even began. It's funny how much has flipped. Mornings have become my favorite part of the day. Waking up fully rested, full of energy, feeling like me—that's a bigger buzz than any drink ever gave me. I saw a book recently called the 5 AM Club. Nope, not for me. 6:30 AM is early enough. But I get the logic. The idea of claiming your free time in the morning instead of wasting it at night makes sense.

Am I becoming boring? Maybe. But in reality, I'm more alert, more productive, more present. And alcohol? It's not even on my mind anymore. It barely takes up 5% of my thoughts, and that's exactly where it needs to be. I'm not resisting temptation, not relying on willpower. It's just... not a thing. I'm thinking about my future instead—how fit I can get, how much better I can feel, and what I can accomplish with all this extra time, money, and energy. For the first time in a long time, I feel optimistic. And that's something alcohol never gave me. Not once.

Alcohol is clever. It tricks you into believing it's helping. It numbs the stress, dulls the pain, and gives you a temporary escape. But in reality, it's just trapping you in a cycle, keeping you stuck. The problems don't go away. They just multiply. And suddenly, you have two problems: whatever was stressing you in the first place and now the added burden of needing alcohol daily just to function. It's a slow, sneaky trap.

The crazy part? I don't even want a drink now. I remember the last time I joined an accountability group on Facebook, posting occasional updates as I went along. The group was full of people struggling to get past day one. I'd see post after post from people who just couldn't start, stuck in a loop of failed attempts. I hate to admit this, but once I was around thirty days sober, I'd look at those posts and think, For God's sake, just do one day. But now I get it. For some people, breaking the cycle is the hardest thing in the world. Myself included.

And I was lucky. Something just clicked this time. It feels simple. Natural. Like I'm finally waking up from a long, heavy sleep. The fog has lifted. The weight is gone. And for the first time in a long time, I can see clearly where I'm going.

The hardest day, as I've said before, is always Day One. The sheer weight of getting through that first sober day can feel overwhelming. It's no wonder, really—everywhere we turn, we're bombarded with the idea that quitting is brutally hard, that withdrawal will be unbearable, and that failure is inevitable. But is it?

Maybe if you drink more than I did, it will be tougher for you. Maybe it won't. Who knows? Not everyone is going to end up shaking in a hospital bed with delirium tremors. That's the end of the spectrum. For many people, breaking the daily cycle is enough to get them through. Once that cycle is broken, sobriety becomes not just possible but manageable. Maybe not forever for everyone, but certainly for long stretches—long enough to remember what life feels like without alcohol dictating every moment.

And here's something to think about—if you ever find yourself too sick to drink, whether it's the flu or some awful stomach bug, use that as your Day One. It still counts. Start from there, build momentum, and watch how quickly the days stack up. At first, it might feel like a struggle, but soon enough, it gets easier. Then easier. And then, one day, it stops being a struggle at all.

That's why this book is called Day One. Because that single day, that one choice, can be the beginning of something massive. A new path. A shift from drowning in self-doubt to stepping into freedom and optimism. If you're still reading this while sipping on a drink, that's fine. Finish it. Start on Monday. Or start tomorrow. But when you do start, commit.

Imagine it—getting through that first day and realizing you're capable of more than you thought. The days will roll by faster than you expect. Try this: think back to exactly one year ago. Where were you? What were you doing? It doesn't seem that long ago, does it? So, imagine yourself one year from now, completely sober. Imagine waking up clear-headed, with no regrets and no exhaustion dragging you down. That future is yours if you want it.

Take a photo of yourself today and save it as "Day One." Look at it. Hold onto it. This is your moment. This is the first step toward an optimistic version of you—the version that doesn't wake up wondering if they nearly ran over a jogger. The version that takes back control.

Day 17

Canal

I'm still listening to The Unexpected Joy of Being Sober by Catherine Gray, and one line has stuck with me more than any other: "My head weather is now made by Pixar rather than Wes Craven." That perfectly sums up how it feels to recover from alcohol. Suddenly, the fog lifts. The fear, anxiety, and chaos that once felt endless start to fade. You begin to see the future clearly, not through a haze of hangovers and regrets but with a sense of optimism.

Yesterday, I joined a few sober support groups on Facebook. I wasn't sure what to expect, but what I found was both heartbreaking and eye-opening. So many people are suffering daily, minute by minute, stuck in a battle they feel they can never win. One comment stood out to me—a man who had been sober for over a year but still fought a relentless power struggle with alcohol. His frustration led him to buy a bottle of beer, swish it around in his mouth, and spit it out, as if trying to prove to himself that he had control. That moment hit me hard.

This is something people don't always understand. Once alcohol is physically out of your system, the battle isn't with your body anymore—it's with your mind. Your brain has been conditioned to believe alcohol is essential. The media, society, and even well-meaning friends and family reinforce the idea that quitting is nearly impossible without iron-clad willpower. That you'll always be "in recovery." That you'll always be fighting temptation, but that's just not true. At least not to me. Not if you allow your brain to rewire itself.

I think about it like this—imagine standing on a bridge, looking down at two canals running side by side. The canal on the left is clear and blue, with neatly trimmed grass banks stretching all the way to the horizon. This is your drinking brain, the one you've traveled down so many times that it's automatic. You step onto the boat, and before you know it, you're drifting off into the familiar. It's easy, predictable. Even if it leads somewhere dark, at least it's a path you know.

The canal on the right is different. Overgrown trees hang low, blocking the view. The water is murky, the path unclear. It looks difficult, even dangerous. This is sobriety. You know deep down it's the better route, the one that leads to freedom, but it feels intimidating. The first time you try to navigate it, progress is painfully slow. It's frustrating. Every instinct tells you to turn back. But you push on. Day by day, the trees start to clear. The water turns blue. The path becomes easier. Meanwhile, the old canal—the one you used to travel without thinking—starts to change. Without use, it becomes murky, neglected, and harder to navigate. And one day, you realize you don't even think about going that way anymore. You simply don't need it. The old Alcohol canal is now closed.

I'm no scientist, but from my own experience—189 days sober—I believe this is how alcohol dependency rewires your brain. Those neural pathways can be redirected. The more you reinforce the sober path, the stronger it becomes. The old one, the one that led to alcohol, weakens until it fades completely.

But what about relaxation? That was one of my biggest questions at the start. How do you unwind after a long day without alcohol? The truth is, once you're free from its grip, you won't feel the need to escape as much—because alcohol itself was likely causing a lot of that stress in the first place. But when I do need to wind down, I've found new ways that work better without the consequences.

Music helps. Audiobooks too. But something that has completely changed the game for me is ASMR. If you're not familiar, it's a sound-based relaxation technique that triggers a tingling sensation in the body. It could be soft whispering, the sound of a hairbrush running through hair, or even the gentle tapping of nails on a surface. Some people love rain sounds;

others prefer the distant crackling of a campfire. There are endless options, and once you find the one that works for you, it's like unlocking a whole new level of relaxation. I highly recommend giving it a try—just search ASMR on YouTube and prepare to go down the rabbit hole.

Since quitting alcohol, my sleep has been incredible. No tossing and turning. No waking up drenched in sweat. No 3 a.m. trips to the bathroom, head pounding, mouth dry. Just a deep, peaceful rest. **As previously mentioned** I've also been using a guided hypnosis track before bed—a free download called Evening Visualization by Jon Gabriel. It's like a full-body relaxation session, melting away every ounce of tension from my forehead to my toes.

Yesterday, I sent it to a coworker who struggles with sleep. We had a private conversation about it at work, and he gave it a shot. This morning, he told me it worked better than anything he'd tried before. He usually wakes up every couple of hours, but last night, he got a solid six hours straight. Said he couldn't even keep his eyes open by the end of it.

That conversation got me thinking. I'm considering asking him to be my sponsor—someone I can turn to if I ever find myself slipping. I trust him to take it seriously and keep our talks private. Having someone like that, someone who gets it could make all the difference.

Looking back at the last 17 days, I realize something: I don't miss alcohol. Not really. I don't miss the hangovers, the regrets, the constant need to "take the edge off" only to wake up feeling worse. I don't waste time thinking about when I can have my next drink. I don't miss the exhaustion. I don't miss the guilt.

What I have now is something alcohol could never give me—clarity, peace, control. The ability to relax without needing a substance. The ability to sleep without interruption. The ability to wake up feeling good, ready to take on the day instead of recovering from the night before.

This is freedom. And it all started with Day One.

I joined a few Facebook groups yesterday, hoping to find one that felt right. But as I scrolled through the posts, I realized something—I'm not sure I want to be in any of them. It's not that I don't appreciate support or understand the value of accountability, but I don't want alcohol to take up space in my thoughts anymore. I don't want it to consume my life.

I remember reading an interview with comedian Billy Connolly when he was first diagnosed with Parkinson's disease. He was asked how he was managing, how the support was going, and what it felt like to be diagnosed. His answer stuck with me. He said he didn't know—because he wasn't thinking about it. He wasn't in any support groups because he didn't want his entire life to revolve around Parkinson's. He didn't want a new set of "Parkinson's friends," and he didn't want every conversation to be about how terrible the disease was. That resonated with me deeply. I think I feel the same way about the Facebook groups I saw yesterday.

That being said, I know that accountability groups help many people. If it works for you, it works—keep doing it. But what I want more than anything for you to understand in this book is that you can be totally free from alcohol. Totally free. Forever.

One of the groups I considered joining required me to post a favorite picture of myself. I hesitated for a moment before choosing one. If you remember, I take a photo of myself every day and write a number next to it, marking my days of sobriety. The picture I chose was from day 188—just one day before I started drinking again after 443 days of "moderating."

Shortly after posting, someone commented: "Congratulations on your sobriety for 188 days." At first, I felt a pang of disappointment. I replied honestly, explaining that I had started drinking again and was now on day 16. They responded that they understood but still thought I should be congratulated for those 189 days of sobriety.

That perspective had never even crossed my mind. All I had felt was disappointment and stupidity. I could remember day 190 so clearly—the first day after I started drinking again. I took a photo, as usual, but while I was drawing the number "190" next to me, I already knew I was going to the pub that evening. I could just feel it.

So, are we ever truly free? I was. For 175 of those 189 days, I was completely free. The first week was tough, and in the days leading up to drinking again, the thoughts of alcohol had crept back in. But in between those moments, I lived. I even went on a family holiday to Spain and didn't drink. I enjoyed it. It pleased me that I didn't need to drink.

Now, I'm getting back to that place again. I've read that it takes most people a few attempts to become sober forever. That means my 189 days of real-life experience should be a massive advantage. Instead of seeing it as a failure, I need to use it as proof that I can do this. That I already have done it. And that I can do it for good.

There's a lesson in this: don't fight the current. Don't run into the wind or swim against the tide. Do what works for you. But try to understand that you don't have to fight alcohol for the rest of your life. You can be free.

And by the way, I've discovered that I really like ear-scratching ASMR. It's surprisingly relaxing.

Day 18

Numb

I'm choking on a bowl of Alpen breakfast cereal as I type this. No more greasy bacon sandwiches needed to soak up last night's alcohol. It's a strange adjustment, really. I don't even like Alpen—it sticks to my teeth—but it's a small price to pay for reclaiming my health.

Reading back over the last eighteen days, I realize I might be coming across as a bit smug. Maybe you're thinking, "Well, this is all so easy for him. My situation is different because of X, Y, or Z." And I get it. The truth is, I do feel a little smug, but only because I remember what it was like on day one. I felt like a complete embarrassment. If you haven't started your day one yet, I urge you to do it. Write down how you feel, record a voice memo, or film yourself if that's easier. You need something to look back on as you move forward. I read my day one diary nearly every day as a reminder of where I started.

There's something else I want to mention—something that used to irritate me when I was still drinking. It was hearing ex-drinkers say, "My life is just better on every level." That phrase used to get under my skin. I was stuck in my routine, drinking every night, and the idea of life being better without alcohol seemed ridiculous. But here's the thing: it's true. And if that annoys you, I completely understand. I used to feel the same way.

I want you to feel smug, too. I want you to enhance your life in ways you never thought possible. I want you to be free. If you've been waiting for a magical genie to grant your wish to be free from alcohol, then consider this your wish granted. I won't sugarcoat it—it hasn't been easy. It's been rough. But things do get easier.

Maybe you're reading this and thinking, "Well, this guy wasn't even really addicted. He only had three or four pints a night." So let me remind you—I went 443 days straight, drinking every single day after a previous sober stretch of 189 days. And here's the thing: it doesn't matter how much you drink. I saw a Facebook post yesterday from a guy who drinks alcohol only once a month, and he absolutely hates himself for it. If alcohol is a problem for him, then it's a problem. If it's a problem for me, it's a problem. The amount doesn't determine the impact.

Right now, I feel elated, and you can too. After spending 443 days trapped in pure exhaustion and misery, it's no wonder I'm feeling the joy of early recovery. I'm going to embrace it and use it as a springboard to improve every aspect of my life.

I remember watching an interview with Monty Python's Eric Idle, where he talked about alcohol. He mentioned having phases of drinking and stopping, saying that it feels good to clean up once in a while. He gave off the impression that he could "take it or leave it." How many times have you heard someone say that? How many times have you said it yourself? I know I have. But let's be real—that phrase is often just a mask, a way to justify drinking.

One of the most fascinating things about quitting alcohol is seeing how people react. Once they notice you looking healthier, they become curious. The first question is always the same: "You not drinking, mate?" And I always reply with the same answer: "Not at the minute, I'm enjoying some time off." Some people nod and move on. Others feel the need to explain why they are drinking and how they can "take it or leave it." But more often than not, people want to know why and how I did it. Deep down, I think most people know they need to cut down or stop drinking, and they're searching for some kind of inside knowledge.

When I used to go to my local pub, I'd usually arrive around 10 p.m. It stayed open until midnight most nights, but only a handful of regulars like me were there. It's no secret that the era of the social pub drinker is dying. Young people just don't do it the same way anymore. But for me, drinking always comes at the end of a productive day. I made sure my work was done, my kids were in bed, or my band rehearsal was over. Then it was time for my "relaxing" drink—or two.

But let's call it what it was. Numbing.

I was numbing my troubles away for a few hours, thinking it was working. And for a while, it did. But the reality is that everyone has stress, grief, regrets, and struggles. And I can tell you from experience that numbing those feelings with alcohol won't solve anything. The only thing that truly helps is facing them head-on.

It's strange looking back now at the way I used to think. I used to believe drinking helped me unwind and that it was a reward for a long day. But what was I actually rewarding myself with? Exhaustion? Guilt? A foggy head the next morning?

These last eighteen days have opened my eyes. I feel more present. More in control. More alive. And I want you to feel that, too. It's not about deprivation—it's about freedom. The freedom to wake up without regrets. The freedom to be fully engaged in life. The freedom to feel everything, good and bad, without numbing it away.

I used to think that sobriety was a sentence, a boring existence where fun and spontaneity went to die. But the truth is, alcohol was the thing killing my spontaneity. It was keeping me stuck.

So, if you're reading this and you haven't started yet, start now. Could you write it down? Record it. Document it in any way that feels natural to you. Because one day, you'll want to look back and see how far you've come. And when you do, you might just feel a little smug, too. And trust me—that's a feeling worth chasing.

Facing problems head-on, or even just speaking openly about what's been weighing on your mind, is always the better option. Alcohol might offer temporary relief, a brief numbing of emotions, but the reality is that it only amplifies the weight of those burdens over time. It lulls you into thinking you're managing, when in truth, you're just pressing pause on problems that will still be there, waiting, once the haze wears off.

For the first time in years, I'm genuinely looking forward to running into someone I haven't seen in a while and having them notice the change—seeing me healthier, sharper, lighter, both in weight and in spirit. I want them to ask how I did it, and I want to tell them the truth. Sobriety didn't just save me; it freed me. And this journey, this story, isn't just about me. It's about anyone who needs to hear that it's possible. That's why I'm writing this—to offer something real, something honest. The truth is, yes, it's hard at first. But the clarity and relief that come with sobriety? That's a rush far greater than anything alcohol ever gave me. And this time, it's real.

Drinking makes it easy to neglect yourself. It makes you forget to eat properly, to move your body, and to care about things that matter. It's a slow erosion of self, and the worst part is you don't even notice it happening. I used to justify my drinking by telling myself I had everything under control—work was done, the kids were in bed, rehearsals were over. Only then would I 'reward' myself with a drink or two. But what was I really doing? Numbing. Avoiding. Convincing myself that drowning in the noise for a few hours was the same as dealing with it.

We all carry something. Grief, regret, heartbreak, missed chances. Some of it can never be undone. Some wounds stay fresh no matter how much time passes. I have my own—things too personal to lay out here—but they weigh heavy. And I know I'm not alone in that. The difference now is that I'm finally facing them. Because I've searched the bottom of a bottle for answers, and I can tell you with certainty: there's nothing there.

There is, however, something on the other side of this. A chance to be free. A chance to take back control, to feel proud, even a little smug, about choosing better for yourself. Do you remember those "Choose Your Own Adventure" books? That's exactly what this is. Your life, your story. And you get to decide where it goes from here. Like they said in The Shawshank Redemption: Get busy living, or get busy dying. I'm choosing to live.

Day 19 - 23

The Clock

Today feels miserable. If I'm being completely honest, the whole weekend has been miserable. Plans I was looking forward to didn't happen, unexpected issues cropped up, and nothing seemed to go the way I wanted. But in the midst of all that, something dawned on me—I never once thought about alcohol. It wasn't my go-to coping mechanism, and that realization hit me harder than the disappointment of the weekend itself. This was just life happening the way it does. No numbing, no escaping, just dealing with it.

One thing did catch my attention last night, though. A TV advert for alcohol-free beer. It made me wonder just how desperate breweries must be if they're all scrambling to create 0% beers and lagers. The last time I spoke to the landlord at my local pub, he admitted—somewhat reluctantly—that the demand for alcohol-free options was through the roof. He had even started serving 0% Guinness, though he wasn't thrilled about it. That got me thinking—what does this shift really mean? There's a change happening in social behavior around alcohol. Maybe more people are questioning their drinking habits. Maybe they just want to blend in at the pub without getting the dreaded "Why aren't you drinking?" interrogation. A pint glass filled with something that looks the part that avoids the awkward conversations, and honestly, that's not a bad thing.

But are alcohol-free beers a good option? For me, the answer isn't so straightforward. Let's be real—when you're addicted to alcohol, you don't go to the pub for the ambiance or the salted peanuts. You go because you need the alcohol. I can't imagine my past self going to the pub 443 days in a row just to sip on a 0% Guinness. The reason people drink is to momentarily numb themselves from the stresses of life, only to ultimately make those same stresses worse thanks to alcohol's depressing effects. For me, I never wanted to hide the fact that I had stopped drinking. I've tried 0% options before. About five years ago, I attempted a few nights of sobriety by drinking Heineken 0.0. For some people, this works. It lets them keep their routine—coming home from work, sitting down with a beer, unwinding—except now, it's alcohol-free.

During my 189 days sober, I bought some 0% lager while on holiday in Spain. It wasn't very good. I took a sip on my balcony one evening, watching people stagger home from their nights out, and immediately regretted it. The taste was foul, but more than that, it felt like I was backsliding. In my mind, it seemed like I was still chasing alcohol, still needing a replacement. That didn't sit well with me. It made me feel like I was missing out on something when, in reality, I wasn't missing anything at all. That's what I want to emphasize—be careful. If you're truly free from alcohol, you don't need a substitute. That being said, in the early days of sobriety, I understand why people turn to alcohol-free options. If you've had multiple failed attempts on day one (and let's be honest, most of us have), maybe a 0% drink could help bridge the gap. If it works for you, then it works. There's no shame in that.

I get a kick out of ordering a soft drink at the pub. A pint of Coca-Cola, a Pepsi—whatever I feel like. I love it when the bartender asks, "It's Pepsi, is that okay?" as if it makes a difference. That phrase alone would make a brilliant marketing campaign. But the real joy? It's knowing I can drink whatever I want, not because I need it, but because I choose it. There's power in that. I'm proud that I don't rely on alcohol anymore.

One of the best parts of being sober is socializing. You become a detective, a people-watcher, and—if I'm being honest—a bit of a sober snob. Something is fascinating about observing a night out with completely clear eyes. One of my favorite experiences was a trip to Blackpool after a band competition.

We had played all afternoon and decided to go out in the evening for food and drinks. The night started great, but as the hours passed, I watched the shift happen. It's mesmerizing, really—the way people change as alcohol takes hold. At first, the drinks flow easily, the conversations are lively, and the laughter comes naturally. Then, the voices get louder; everyone starts talking over each other, competing to be heard. Eventually, the night takes a turn—the arguments start, the laughter fades, and the reality of alcohol sets in.

I remember sitting back, completely sober, and realizing how much I used to be part of that cycle—the high energy, the slurred words, the exaggerated emotions. It was all so familiar, but this time, I wasn't in it. I was watching it unfold from the outside, and I felt something unexpected—relief. Relief that I didn't need it anymore. Relief that I wouldn't wake up the next morning full of regret, piecing together hazy memories and nursing a hangover.

This is the part they don't tell you about sobriety. It's not just about not drinking. It's about seeing the world differently and experiencing life in a way you never could before. It's about stepping out of the cycle and realizing you don't need it. That's freedom. And I wouldn't trade it for anything.

What struck me most that night wasn't just how predictable the cycle was but how detached I felt from it. There was no anxiety about when my next drink would arrive or whether I was drinking fast enough before the last order. No frantic calculations about who owed the next round. I simply enjoyed the company, had real conversations, and when I'd had enough, I made a decision no one in my past drinking days would have even considered—I left. It was around 11 p.m., and I realized there was no real reason for me to stay. My car was with me, I was completely sober, and my home was **just a short drive away.** By 1 a.m., I was back in my bed, and the next morning, I was up early, refreshed, and out for the day with my family.

The contrast became even clearer when I saw the aftermath. Photos and stories of the previous night trickled in, along with complaints about pounding headaches, sickness, and regret. Some were still too hungover to even think about heading home. That's when sobriety felt like a superpower. I had experienced the night, laughed, socialized, and walked away from it all with nothing but good memories—no shame, no sickness, no wasted day recovering.

I've come to enjoy socializing sober genuinely. At first, it was a little strange, and yes, there were questions— "Why aren't you drinking?"—but after a while, people stopped asking. And honestly, it became fun watching others panic about last orders or scramble to finish a drink before moving to the next pub.

I've been there. I know the feeling all too well—that quiet desperation of trying to fit in just one more drink before the night ends. I've seen bandmates rushing to load instruments into the van, constantly checking the time, and anxious about making it to the pub before closing. That fear of missing out wasn't even about the night itself; it was about the drink. The drink was always the priority. Alcohol ties you to the clock.

One conversation that stuck with me was with a guy who was planning a trip to Walt Disney World with his family and some friends. He proudly told me how he forced everyone up early to get to the theme parks before the crowds arrived. It made sense—those parks are overwhelming in the afternoons. But when I asked him what he thought about the incredible evening shows, the fireworks, and the way the entire place transforms at night, he had no idea. He had never seen them. Every evening of his trip, he had been in the pub. That was his priority, and he didn't even realize what he was missing. Alcohol addiction forced him to make time for those drinks.

And that's the thing—when you're caught up in drinking, you don't think about what it's taking from you. You convince yourself you're living life, but in reality, you're structuring everything around alcohol. I know because I did it, too. Family outings were never just about spending time together; in the back of my mind, I was always calculating how long we had before I needed to be back at the pub. It wasn't a conscious choice—it just was. That's how addiction works.

Now, that weight is gone. There's no internal countdown, no pressure, no invisible chain pulling me toward the next drink. I get to be fully present, fully aware, fully free. And that's a feeling I wouldn't trade for anything.

Day 24- 30

Berts silence

So here I am—30 days sober. I know what you might be thinking: "That's just Dry January." And you're right. But let's be honest, 30 days without alcohol is no small feat. More importantly, it has given me something I didn't fully expect—freedom. I opened the door to alcohol years ago, and for the longest time, it felt impossible to close it. But here's what I've learned: even seven days without drinking can truly change your life. If you're reading this, I hope the methods in this book help you keep your version of "Bert" locked away, just like I have.

Right now, my Bert is nothing more than an empty shell at the bottom of his box. If he were a plush teddy, all his stuffing would be pulled out. In the beginning, he was aggressive—haunting me in my dreams, screaming at me to give in and pour a drink. But after 30 days? Silence. He's powerless. And I'm in control. I'm not missing out, I'm not substituting alcohol with something else, and I'm certainly not going through this "one day at a time." I'm done. Completely don

Golden Rules

Staying sober isn't just about willpower; it's about having a plan. So, here are the golden rules that helped me get here and will help you, too:

1. Commit to Day One. It doesn't matter how many times you've tried and failed—today is a fresh start. Write down how alcohol has been controlling your life and what you hope to gain by quitting. Record a video or audio message to yourself, something raw and honest. Capture this moment. Take a photo of yourself and label it "Day 1." Make it real. Make it count.

2. Create your own "Bert." Give your cravings a ridiculous character—a Womble, an Oompa Loompa, anything silly. The point is to externalize your addiction and make it something you can control. Picture yourself stuffing your version of Bert into a bag, locking him away, watching him shrink. You hold the power—not him.

3. Watch Cast Away. When Tom Hanks rows away from that island, he knows he's free, no matter what challenges lie ahead. That's you, leaving alcohol behind. No more being stranded.

https://www.youtube.com/watch?v=7w8KVXvgsFw

4. Remember that someone loves you. There is at least one person in this world who wants you to live your best, sober life. Think of them when things get tough.

5. Find what works for you. If non-alcoholic drinks help, great. If it's walking, even better. Just do something. Move. Even if it's just ten minutes a day.

6. Tell someone. Share your journey with a trusted friend or family member. Ask if you can reach out when you're struggling. Accountability matters.

7. Don't try to moderate. Seriously, don't. Moderation is the ultimate trap. If I could give just one piece of advice, this would be it.

8. Be kind to yourself. This isn't easy. Talk to yourself like you would talk to a friend who's going through the same thing.

9. Own your sobriety. Society makes us justify not drinking, which is absurd. Be proud of your choice. You don't owe anyone an explanation.

10. Accept that the beginning is the hardest. You're carving out a new path, like digging a canal. It takes time, but once it's open, everything flows easier.

11. Flip the script. Fill your world with positive influences. Follow sober influencers on social media, listen to

recovery audiobooks, and surround yourself with inspiration.

12. Get professional help if needed. There's no shame in seeking support. A therapist, counselor, or support group can make all the difference.
13. Stay busy. Identify your trigger times and have a plan. Don't leave space for temptation to creep in.
14. Prioritize sleep. A well-rested mind is a strong mind. Go to bed earlier and make sleep a priority.
15. Use hypnotic audio. Find a relaxation audio or meditation that resonates with you. Let your shoulders drop, breathe deeply, and learn to relax without alcohol.
16. Beware of the "honeymoon is over" phase. The novelty of sobriety can wear off. If thoughts of drinking return, recognize them, get busy, and go to bed early if needed.
17. Forgive yourself for past attempts. If you've tried and failed before, that's okay. Every attempt brought you here. And when you truly feel free, you'll know it.
18. Remember, this is YOUR journey. People who have been through it admire those in the early stages. You're doing something brave and worthwhile.

19. Plan your sober future. What will you do with all the extra time, energy, and money you used to spend on drinking? Dream big and take action.
20. Pass it on. If this book has helped you, share it with someone who might need it. Sobriety is a gift—don't keep it to yourself.

Thirty days ago, I wasn't sure I could do this. Now, I can't imagine going back. I don't feel deprived. I don't feel like I'm missing out. I feel free. And the best part? You can, too.

Conclusion

Thirty days. One month. Four weeks. However you choose to count it, I've made it—30 days alcohol-free.

I know what you might be thinking and I get it. But if you've ever tried quitting something that had its claws in you, you'll understand—this is a big deal. Not because I'm perfect, not because I have some superhuman willpower, but because I'm just a regular guy who finally took control.

I won't lie—this journey hasn't been easy. In the beginning, my cravings were loud, relentless, and intrusive. It felt like "Bert," my personified addiction, was screaming at me to give in. He invaded my dreams, whispered excuses in my ear, and convinced me that drinking was the only way to feel normal. But now? He's nothing more than a deflated plush toy at the bottom of his box, lifeless, powerless. I have the control, and I'm free.

What I've learned over these past 30 days is that you don't have to be perfect to break free—you just have to start. Even if you've failed before, even if you think you can't do it, you can.

I've realized that the hardest part of quitting is simply getting through day one. But once you do that? Everything changes.

If you take just one thing from this book, let it be this: you have more power over your addiction than you think. No one else can do this for you. No one can shove "Bert" into his box but you. But once you do, life on the other side is better than you can imagine.

So, if you're reading this, if you've made it this far, I hope you take action. I hope you try, even if you stumble. And I hope you realize that a life without alcohol isn't about missing out—it's about finally living.

That's it from me. If you're looking for more resources or support, visit https://soberdayone.com/ or https://www.facebook.com/groups/soberdayone.

Now, if you'll excuse me, I've got some toenails to cut.

Paul Stamp.

Printed in Great Britain
by Amazon